Nelson

Handwriting

Pupil Book 4

Nelson

Look at these letters.

Lower case letters for handwriting

a b c d e f g h i j k l m n
o p q r s t u v w x y z

Lower case print letters

a b c d e f g h i j k l m n
o p q r s t u v w x y z

Capital letters

A B C D E F G H I J K L M
N O P Q R S T U V W X Y Z

The joined alphabet

abcdefghijklmnopqrstuvwxyz

Copy the letters.
Check your writing against the page.

Remember to slope your
writing slightly to the
right.

Look at these numerals.

1 2 3 4 5 6 7 8 9 0

Copy the numerals.
Now copy these subtractions and write the answers.

32345	98765	24680	97531
-16789	-43210	-13579	-86420

Now copy these words to practise making the joins

The first join
Set 1 to Set 2

in

in indeed inside instinct
under undid unite up

The second join
Set 1 to Set 3

ak

cake deck mail make
sail stick take trail

The third join
Set 4 to Set 2

fa

fall frock over river
vole wreck write wrong

The fourth join
Set 4 to Set 3

ok

broke joke off roll
stroke troll what while

The break letters

elephant foxes girl jam
jumbo year quick zoo

A project should be thoughtfully planned.
It might include:

- a list of contents   • tables of information
- written accounts   • poems
- illustrations

Present your project in your best handwriting so that others will enjoy reading it.

Class 6 was doing a project about Charles Darwin, the famous scientist.
Copy their list of contents.

1 Table of important events

2 The life of Charles Darwin

3 Scientific investigations

4 Research into the hearing of worms

Copy this table.

Table of Important Events

1809 Born in Shrewsbury, England

1831 Sailed to South America on
            HMS Beagle

1839 Journal of his voyage published

1859 "The Origin of Species" published

1882 Died

Now copy this account.

The Life of Charles Darwin

Charles Darwin was born in 1809 in Shrewsbury. He studied Theology at the University of Cambridge but became very interested in Natural History, the study of plants, animals and rocks. He wrote several books including an important one called "The Origin of Species". This explained his ideas about the way in which animal and plant species change gradually through the centuries. Charles Darwin died in 1882.

Copy this information, putting in the capital letters and full stops.

Scientific Investigations in South America, Darwin explored the Brazilian jungle he measured earthquake damage in the Andes mountains and he studied interesting creatures he also studied animal life on the Galapagos Islands and in Australia these are some of the animals he investigated

South American animals

Armadillo
Darwin's Finch
Darwin's Frog
Darwin's Lizard

Australian animals

Crimson Rosella
Duck-billed Platypus
Pink Cockatoo
Rat Kangaroo

Now copy this information.

Research into the Hearing of Worms

In a book called "On Humus and Earthworms", Darwin described some of his experiments on worms:

"They took not the least notice of the shrill notes from a metal whistle... nor did they of the deepest and loudest notes of a bassoon. When placed on a table close to the keys of a piano, which was played as loudly as possible, they remained perfectly quiet. However, when the note C in the bass clef was struck, they instantly retreated into their burrows."

When we add *mis* or *dis* to the beginning of some verbs, it gives them the opposite meaning.

behave   misbehave   agree disagree

Copy each of these verbs neatly.
Then write a verb with the opposite meaning by adding *mis* or *dis*.

1 understand   2 obey   3 appear

4 lead   5 govern   6 mount

7 connect   8 pronounce 9 count

10 agree   11 behave   12 allow

Now make a chart like this.
Write each of the verbs in the correct column.

mis	dis

Take care when joining from *s*.

8

Copy each of these sentences. Using the word in brackets, write another sentence which means the same. The first one has been done for you.

1. If you are not able to hear someone properly, you may not understand what they say. (misunderstand)

   If you are not able to hear someone properly, you may misunderstand what they say.

2. The soldiers did not obey their orders. (disobeyed)

3. When you are learning a new language, you do not pronounce some words properly. (mispronounce)

4. Tom did not agree with Sam. (disagreed)

5. Kylie counted wrongly when she checked the pencils. (miscounted)

Practice with word origins

Many English words come from Latin words.
In Latin, *specto* means *I watch*. The word *spectator* comes from this.

There were lots of
spectators at the match.

Copy this chart.

Latin word	Meaning	English words
habito	I live	inhabit habitat
video	I see	vision visible
audio	I hear	audible audience
porto	I carry	porter transport
scribo	I write	describe manuscript
facio	I make	manufacture factory

Can you add any more
English words to your chart?

Copy the sentences. After each sentence, write the Latin word from which the underlined word comes.

1   Her voice was so quiet that it was hardly <u>audible</u>.

2   The <u>porter</u> carried our bags to our room.

3   The telescopes were made in a small <u>factory</u> in Switzerland.

4   When I got my new glasses my <u>vision</u> was much better.

5   The rainforest is the <u>habitat</u> of many colourful birds.

6   The archaeologist found an ancient <u>manuscript</u> hidden in the cave.

How are you getting on?
Look at the checklist.
Keep practising!

Some words are not spelled as you would expect.

cupboard

shepherd

Write these words.
Underline the tricky part or parts of each word.

1 library   2 neighbour   3 government

4 miniature   5 antique   6 orchestra

Copy these definitions.
Choose one of the words above to go with each definition.

1 _____ someone living nearby

2 _____ a group of musicians

3 _____ very small

4 _____ a group of people who
make the laws

5 _____ a collection of books

6 _____ old and valuable

Some people make up silly sentences to help them to remember tricky spellings.

skeleton

Don't <u>let on</u> that you saw a ske<u>let</u>on!

Copy these silly sentences to help you.

1 necessary   <u>N</u>ever <u>e</u>at <u>c</u>abbage; <u>e</u>at <u>s</u>lug <u>s</u>andwiches <u>a</u>nd <u>r</u>emain <u>y</u>oung.

2 island   An <u>island</u> is <u>land</u> surrounded by water.

3 favourite   "Favourite" is <u>our</u> fav<u>our</u>ite word.

4 temperature   A high <u>temper</u>ature has a bad <u>temper</u>.

5 separate   Don't get se<u>parat</u>ed from your <u>para</u>chute.

Think of some words that you find tricky to spell.
Write a silly sentence for each to help you to remember the spelling.

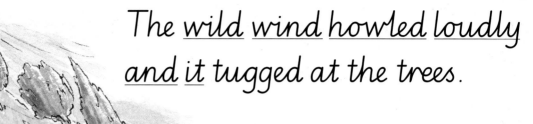

The <u>wild</u> <u>wind</u> <u>howled</u> <u>loudly</u> <u>and</u> <u>it</u> tugged at the trees.

wild	an adjective	wind	a noun
howled	a verb	loudly	an adverb
and	a conjunction	it	a pronoun

Copy this story.

A <u>fierce</u> <u>lion</u> <u>escaped</u> from <u>his</u> <u>cage</u>. <u>He</u> <u>chased</u> a <u>small</u> <u>girl</u> <u>and</u> her <u>big</u> <u>brother</u>. <u>They</u> were very frightened <u>but</u> were <u>soon</u> saved by a <u>brave</u> <u>policeman</u>.

Make a chart like this.
Write each of the underlined words in the correct column.

Noun	Pronoun	Adjective	Verb	Adverb	Conjunction
lion	his	fierce	escaped	soon	and

Copy each of these sentences.
Complete the line underneath each one.

1 In PE we run, jump, hop and skip.
The 4 verbs are _____

2 Sam wore a long blue skirt and her black
hair was tied back in a dark red ribbon.
The 5 adjectives are _____

3 My favourite presents were a football,
a torch and an atlas.
The 4 nouns are _____

4 She said, "Give it to me. It is mine and
you cannot have it."
The 7 pronouns are _____

5 Raza can come now but Ben can't come
until he's finished his homework.
The 2 conjunctions are _____

Punctuation marks are important in writing. They help to make the meaning clear.

"Listen! What's that?" Ben asked.

"It's only the cat," Sam replied.

. full stop   , comma   " " inverted commas

don't apostrophe   *?* question mark   *!* exclamation mark

Copy each of these sentences.
In the space, write the name of the punctuation mark which is being described.

1 *A _____ is used to show readers where to pause, to separate words in a list or to separate words spoken in direct speech from the rest of the sentence.*

2 *An _____ is used to show ownership or to show that letters have been left out.*

Write a sentence about each of the other punctuation marks.

Copy this passage carefully.
Notice the punctuation.

Ben's Mum said, "I've made a packed lunch for you."

"Can't we take some cold sausages?" Ben asked.

"We could take some crisps too," Sam added, "and some biscuits."

Ben looked in the bag. "Oh, good !" he exclaimed. "There's some fizzy drink!"

Rewrite the next part of the story.
Punctuate it correctly.

where shall we go
sam asked ben said lets go to the beach no
said sam Id rather go to the
adventure playground
what a good idea agreed ben

Remember to start a new
line each time a new
person speaks.

People have puzzled over the mystery of the Loch Ness monster for years. Some people claim to have seen it, and there are photographs said to prove that it exists. However, most people doubt that such a creature lives in the Loch.

Similarly, explorers in Asia claim to have seen a tall creature living in the snowy wastes. This is the creature we know as the Abominable Snowman.

A paragraph is a group of sentences about one main idea. Notice how each paragraph starts on a new line and is indented.

Write this information neatly as two paragraphs.
The first paragraph is about how people have described the Abominable Snowman, and the second is about a Yeti hunt.

The Abominable Snowman, also known as the Yeti, is said to be a huge, hairy, human-like creature living in the snows of the Himalayas. In 1957, an explorer went on a Yeti hunt. He didn't find one, but local people told him that five people had been killed by the Yeti in the past four years.

Copy the rest of the account in three paragraphs. The first paragraph is about photographing footprints, and the last is about the way thin air affects the imagination.

In 1951, a mountain climber took photographs of some giant footprints in the snow. They were obviously the footprints of a huge creature, walking on two legs! Or were they? An expert on mountain snow explained that small footprints, possibly from other climbers, could have started to melt in the midday sun and frozen again at night. As the snow melted and then froze again, the footprints would have got bigger and bigger until they looked like monster footprints. High in the mountains, the air is very thin. The lack of oxygen sometimes makes people imagine strange things.

Did you indent all three paragraphs?

KEEP OFF
THE GRASS

Carefully written print is
easy to read.

Print these instructions for making a compass on a piece of paper.

Equipment – bar magnet, string, paper, tape

1   Tie one end of the string round the magnet.

2   Fix the string to the edge of a table.

3   Draw a large circle marked N, S, W, E.

4   Place the paper under the magnet.

5   Turn the paper so that the magnet points
to N.

6   Tape the paper to the floor.

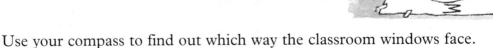

Use your compass to find out which way the classroom windows face.

Give your instructions to a friend in another class.
See if he or she can follow the instructions.

Handwritten menus are often printed to make them easy to read.
Copy these items from the menu in an Italian hotel.
The menu is printed in four languages:
1 Italian   2 French   3 English   4 German

A 1 Tubetti ai frutti di mare
2 Les pâtes aux fruits de mer
3 Seafood pasta
4 Nudeln mit meersfrüchte soße

B 1 Filetto di sogliola dorato
2 Le filet de sole doré
3 Fillet of sole, floured and fried
4 Seezunge Filets paniert und gebacken

C 1 Pollo alla diavola
2 Le poulet grillé à la crapaudine
3 Devilled spring chicken
4 Hühnchen auf teufelsart

Which meal would you order?

Print these instructions for the game Word Chain on a piece of paper.

1 Choose a category, for example, animals.

2 The first player gives a word that fits the category.

3 The second player must give a word that starts with the last letter of the first player's word, and so on.

Example

First player's word	- deer
Second player's word	- rabbit
Third player's word	- tortoise

4 The game continues until a player fails to think of a word that fits and is, therefore, out. The winner is the player who is still in when all the others are out.

Try playing this game with some friends.

Now print this recipe for Spanish omelette on a piece of paper.

Ingredients:
2 boiled potatoes (chopped)
2 teaspoons of onion (chopped)
2 small tomatoes (chopped)
a few peas
50 grams of butter or margarine
4 eggs (beaten)
4 tablespoons of water
Salt and pepper

Method:
1 Butter a foil dish
2 Put vegetables in dish
3 Beat eggs, add water and seasoning
4 Pour mixture over vegetables
5 Bake at Regulo 6 (400°F or 204°C) for 20 minutes or until set

Describe how to make the omelette in complete sentences.

Take your recipe home.
See if an adult can follow it.

Writing with a straight-edged nib is a good way of presenting handwriting.

This sentence was written with a pen with a rounded tip. All the lines are the same thickness.

This sentence was written with a straight - edged nib and so there are both thick and thin strokes.

Read these rules for using a straight-edged nib.

1 Hold your pen lightly about 3cm from the tip.
2 Be sure that the edge of the nib always lies flat on the paper.
3 Keep the nib at the same angle.

You can make three different strokes with a straight-edged nib.

Uphill strokes	Downhill strokes	Medium vertical strokes
/////////	\\\\\\\\\\	∣∣∣∣∣∣∣
are used mainly for joins.	are the thick parts of letters.	are for vertical letters: *i t l*

Practise these patterns and letters with your straight-edged nib.

mmmmm   mmmmm   mmmmm

n n n n n   nnnnnnnn   n n n n n

m m m m   mmmmm   m m m m

h h h h h   hhhhhhhh   h h h h h

k k k k k   kkkkkkkk   k k k k k

uuuuuuu   uuuuuuu   uuuuuuu

u u u u u   uuuuuuu   u u u u u

y y y y y   y y y y y   y y y y y

ccccccc   ccccccc   ccccccc

a a a a a   aaaaaaaa   a a a a a

d d d d d   dddddddd   d d d d d

g g g g g   g g g g g   g g g g g

o o o o o   oooooooo   o o o o o

q q q q q   q q q q q   q q q q q

Did you remember to keep the nib flat and at the same angle all the time?

Penmanship

The width of the thick downhill stroke depends on the nib you use:

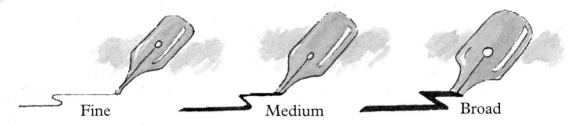

Fine   Medium   Broad

This was written with a fine nib.
This was written with a medium nib.
This was written with a broad nib.

Practise writing with nibs of different widths to see which you prefer.

This sentence was written with a medium nib.
Copy the sentence.

If the straight edge of the nib is always flat on the paper, the uphill strokes will be thin and the downhill strokes will be thick as they are in this sentence.

How are you getting on?
Look at the checklist.
Keep practising!

Practise writing capital letters with a straight-edged nib.

A B C D E F G H I J K L M N
O P Q R S T U V W X Y Z

Now copy this certificate.

CERTIFICATE
OF OUTSTANDING BRAVERY
AWARDED TO BEN

(AN EXCELLENT GUIDE DOG AND A GOOD FRIEND)

FOR SAVING HIS OWNER
WHEN A RUNAWAY LORRY
MOUNTED THE PAVEMENT

Now make a certificate for a firefighter who rescued a child
from a burning house.

Practise writing the numerals with your straight-edged nib.

0 1 2 3 4 5 6 7 8 9

This chart is called the Beaufort Scale.
It measures the strength of the wind.
Copy the chart.

Did you remember to keep the nib flat on the paper so that your numerals had thick and thin parts?

Beaufort Number	Wind	Speed in m.p.h.
0	calm	less than 1
1	light air	1 – 3
2	light breeze	4 – 7
3	gentle breeze	8 – 12
4	moderate breeze	13 – 18
5	fresh breeze	19 – 24
6	strong breeze	25 – 31
7	moderate gale	32 – 38
8	fresh gale	39 – 46
9	strong gale	47 – 54
10	whole gale	55 – 63
11	storm	64 – 75
12	hurricane	above 75

Use your straight-edged nib to copy these verses.

Wind

Wind is to show
How a thing can blow,
And especially through trees.
When it is fast
It is called a blast,
And it's otherwise known as a breeze.

Blow down a pine,
Clothes from a line,
Tumble a chimney top.
Wind is the general sound
You hear around,
That suddenly likes to stop.

by Leonard Feeney

Everyone's handwriting is different.
Even children who have been taught the same style develop individuality in their writing.

On Monday, which is Good Friday,

There will be a mothers' meeting for
fathers only

You prepare a table for me
in the presence of my enemies.

Great fleas have little fleas upon their backs to bite 'em,
And little fleas have lesser fleas and so on ad infinitum.

Sand in your fingernails
sand between your toes
Sand in your earholes
Sand up your nose!

Leave your Supper and leave your Sleep,
Come with your playfellows into the Street,

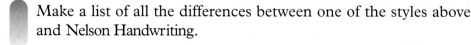

Make a list of all the differences between one of the styles above and Nelson Handwriting.

Some children decide to make joins after the letters
b and *p* because it speeds up their handwriting.

In Nelson Handwriting *b* and
p are break letters.

Compare these two examples.

Bobby likes pears and apples
but Poppy prefers blackberries.

Bobby likes pears and apples
but Poppy prefers blackberries.

Copy the second example.
You may need to have several tries to get used to
joining after *b* and *p*.

Are you pleased with the
extra joins?

Now copy this verse, remembering to join after *p*.

In the Shrovetide
pancake races,
pancake experts
show their paces.
Pancakes dropped
or held aloft,
Pancakes proud,
Pancakes flopped.

by Ann Bonner

Developing an individual style

Other children decide to introduce loops to speed up their writing.

There are no loops in Nelson Handwriting.

Compare these three examples of looped writing. Copy them carefully.

1

There was a young lady of Ryde
Who ate a green apple and died.

Example 1 has loops to the ascenders.

2

There was a young lady of Ryde
Who ate a green apple and died.

Example 2 has loops from the descenders.

3

There was a young lady of Ryde
Who ate a green apple and died.

Where are the loops in Example 3?

Now copy the whole limerick in Style 3.
You will need to practise.

There was a young lady of Ryde
Who ate a green apple and died.
The apple fermented
Inside the lamented
And made cider inside her inside.

Other children add flourishes to their capital letters.

M A H F

This poem has been written with flourishes on capital letters, loops to ascenders and from descenders and joins after *b* and *p*.
Copy it in the style of writing you prefer.

If you decide to join from *b* and *p*, or add loops or flourishes to your writing, make sure it is still easy to read.

Motor Cars

From a city window, way up high,
I like to watch the cars go by.
They look like burnished beetles,
                    black,
That leave a little muddy track
Behind them as they slowly
                    crawl.
Sometimes they do not move at all,
But huddle close with hum
                    and drone,
As though they feared to be
                    alone.
They grope their way through
                    fog and night
With the golden feelers of
                    their light.

by Rowena Bennett

33

A simile describes something by comparing it to something similar. Similes often begin with *as* or *like*.

I'm <u>as hungry as a wolf</u>.

Copy these similes.

1 as quiet as a mouse   2 as happy as a lark

3 as blind as a bat   4 as agile as a monkey

5 as bright as a button   6 as strong as an ox

7 as fresh as a daisy   8 as heavy as lead

Choose a suitable word from the brackets to complete each of these similes. Write them neatly.

1 as steady as a _____   (book, rock, jelly)

2 as slow as a _____   (hare, mouse, tortoise)

3 as cold as _____   (ice, custard, pasta)

4 as green as _____   (cabbage, a tree, grass)

Copy these sentences.
Decide on a suitable simile to complete each one.
Underline the similes.

1 The pirate looked fierce, but he was really
   as gentle as a _____.

2 Mrs. Smith's hat was as flat as a _____ after
   Mrs. Broadbent sat on it.

3 The detective never seemed to panic.
   He was as cool as a _____.

4 The queen's eyes sparkled like _____.

5 The weightlifter was as strong as an _____.

6 The noisy express train hurtled through
   the station like a _____.

7 The motorway stretched ahead of us,
   as straight as an _____.

8 The clouds floated gently by like _____.

How are you getting on?
Look at the checklist.
Keep practising!

A figure of speech is a colourful way of expressing something.

Nathan <u>got into hot water</u> when he smashed the window.
(got into trouble)

Copy these figures of speech
Write what each one means.

1 To hold your tongue – To keep quiet
2 To blow your own trumpet
3 To hit the nail on the head
4 To have your heart in your mouth
5 To bury the hatchet
6 To show a clean pair of heels
7 To throw dust in someone's eyes
8 To smell a rat

Here are five more figures of speech.

1 To turn over a new leaf
2 To put the cart before the horse
3 To let the cat out of the bag
4 To turn the tables
5 To rain cats and dogs

Copy each of these sentences and choose a figure of speech from the list above to describe the situation.

1 Gemma was told to keep the surprise party a secret but she forgot and told some of the other children. To let the cat out of the bag.

2 The storm was so bad that the drains overflowed and puddles lay everywhere.

3 The red team lost every time they played the blue team until this week when they won.

4 Amy was always in trouble and her parents said that she must start behaving better.

5 Jamie brushed his teeth and then ate a huge bar of chocolate.

If you are writing a story, you need to follow this action plan.

<u>Brainstorm</u>

the theme (main idea)
the plot (beginning, middle and end)
the characters (people)
the setting (place)

<u>Draft the beginning</u>
Introduce theme, characters, setting

<u>Revise and edit the beginning</u>

<u>Draft the middle</u>
Describe actions and events

<u>Revise and edit the middle</u>

<u>Draft the ending</u>
Describe how things turn out

<u>Revise and edit the ending</u>

<u>Write the final version</u>

Write the final version neatly so others will enjoy your story.

Copy the action plan.

This is Daniel's draft of the beginning and the middle of a story.
He has started to edit it by underlining the words he wants to change.

Bruce to the Rescue

Eleven year-old Stuart was on a hill walk with two older boys, Kieran and Adam. He had had to promise his mum that he wouldn't go swimming in the cold streams. The boys were walking in the hills near their village in Scotland. It was spring and squirrels were <u>running</u> everywhere. The trees were <u>coming</u> into bud. A stray dog called Bruce followed them, <u>moving</u> excitedly here and there and sniffing the <u>smells</u>.

When they were almost back at their village they had a <u>surprise</u>. The bridge they were expecting to cross had been <u>taken</u> away by the stream.

Adam said, "We'll have to swim across."

Poor Stuart! He <u>knew</u> his promise, but what could he do?

Make a list of the underlined words and the ones you would choose to improve the story.

running – scampering

Can you improve the passage even more? Write the new version neatly.

Now draft and edit an ending for the story.

Practice with play scripts

The story in a play is told through the speeches of the characters, set out like this.

Robin: Stand back and let the better man cross!

Stranger: I AM the better man, so get out of my way!

Copy the next part of the play.

Robin: Do you want my arrow in your ribs?

Stranger: You talk like a coward.

Robin: I am no coward. No man has ever called
                   me one.

Stranger: You are a coward. You have a bow and
                   arrow. I have nothing to fight with except
                   my staff.

Robin: I'll throw away my arrows and cut a staff
                   from the forest, then we'll be even.

Copy the next part of the play. Write the missing words.

Robin: _____

Stranger: _____

Robin: So you want a drink of water, do you,
            stranger? I'm ready and I'll strike.

Stranger: I don't call that a strike. Take that!

Robin: And you take that! How now! Where have
            you gone?

Stranger: I am right HERE! Take that, and down you
            go into the water.

Carry on with the play in your own words.

Unit 16 *Presentation*

Take pride in presenting your writing attractively.

Try:
- writing on plain paper
- leaving wide margins
- adding flourishes
- decorating the capitals
- adding patterned borders
- writing inside a shape
- curving the lines of writing

Copy this poem.
Make it look as attractive as you can.

Corroboree

The clap, clap, clap of the clapsticks beat
By the old red rocks with their scars,
To the stamp, stamp, stamp of the old men's feet
And the wink, wink, wink of the stars.

With the drone, drone, drone of the didgeridoo
And the sound of its ancient tune,
In the dance of the snake and the kangaroo,
By the light of the walkabout moon.

by Max Fatchen

Copy this poem carefully.
Notice the shape of the poem.
Does it remind you of the way seals move?

Seal

See how he dives

From the rocks with a zoom!

See how he darts

Through his watery room,

Past crabs and eels

And green seaweed,

Past fluffs of sandy

Minnow feed!

See how he swims

With a swerve and a twist,

A flip of the flipper,

A flick of the wrist!

Quicksilver-quick,

Softer than spray,

Down he plunges

And sweeps away.

by William Jay Smith

Presentation

Haiku is a form of poetry which comes from Japan. A haiku is a three-line poem which should create a vivid picture in the mind.

Copy these examples of haiku.

The Garden Pond

Goldfish shimmering
And dragonflies hovering,
It's warm by the pond.

A Summer Day

Summer sun blazing,
Relaxed in my garden chair,
Just the life for me.

Try writing a haiku.
Think carefully about presentation.

Copy this description of Gollum.
Add some drawings or decorative borders.

Deep down here by the dark water
lived old Gollum, a small slimy
creature. I don't know where he came
from, nor who or what he was. He was
a Gollum – as dark as darkness, except
for two big round pale eyes in his thin
face. He had a little boat, and he rowed
about quite quietly on the lake; for lake
it was, wide and deep and deadly cold.

from The Hobbit by J.R.R. Tolkien

Presentation

People sometimes advertise things they want to sell in the window of a local shop. The best presented advert attracts the most attention.

Choose one of these adverts to copy.
Print the words to make them easy to read.

FOR SALE
1 skateboard
-strong but lightweight
-as good as new
- only one owner
Cost £55 new but will
accept £20 or near offer
Phone 579384

FOR SALE
1 large Victorian dolls' house
complete with furniture
including garden table and chairs
Cost £70
Owner will consider £30 o.n.o.
Phone 576312

Now write an advert for either a doll's pram or a go-kart.

Remember to plan the layout and to write neatly.

Odd One Out

Three of the four words in each row have something in common. Copy each row, find the odd one out and say what the other three have in common.

Set your work out neatly in rows and columns.

1 lady   woman   boy   girl

boy – the others are female

2 car   lorry   tractor   aeroplane

3 tree   book   envelope   cupboard

4 cod   robin   whale   porpoise

5 three   half   quarter   tenth

6 giraffe   lion   ostrich   elephant

7 five   four   three   seven

8 hexagon   triangle   oval   octagon

9 parsnip   potato   apple   carrot

10 Mars   Jupiter   Moon   Saturn

11 parsley   thyme   rosemary   tomato

12 winter   summer   jump   spring

13 lamb   chick   bull   kitten

14 pencil   paintbrush paper   pen

How well have you done? Look at the checklist. Keep practising!

You have come to the end of Pupil Book 4 and the end of the series.
This is a good time to check your progress.

Copy these verses in your best handwriting.

A Calendar

January brings the snow,
Makes our feet and fingers glow.

February brings the rain,
Thaws the frozen lake again.

Copy this verse legibly as many times as you can in three minutes.

March brings breezes loud and shrill,
To stir the dancing daffodil.

Write these verses neatly in your preferred individual style.

April brings the primrose sweet,
Scatters daisies at our feet.

May brings flocks of pretty lambs
Skipping by their fleecy dams.

by Sara Coleridge